GUITAR

MAKING ♪ MUSIC

KATE RIGGS

CREATIVE EDUCATION • CREATIVE PAPERBACKS

PUBLISHED *by* Creative Education
and Creative Paperbacks
P.O. Box 227, Mankato, Minnesota 56002
Creative Education and Creative Paperbacks are
imprints of The Creative Company
www.thecreativecompany.us

DESIGN AND PRODUCTION *by* Ellen Huber
ART DIRECTION *by* Rita Marshall
PRINTED *in* Malaysia

PHOTOGRAPHS *by*
123rf (Nattapon Wongwean), Alamy (Michael Winters),
Bigstock (vkoletic), Corbis (Steve Roche/Demotix),
Dreamstime (Jlye, Oranhall), Getty Images (Mick Hutson/
Redferns, Sir Peter Lely, Jonnie Miles), iStockphoto
(Ela Kwasniewski, David H. Lewis, pixhook, pixitive,
Vladimir Tarasov, tunart, wbgorex), Shutterstock (Andrey
Armyagov, dean bertoncelj, Christian Draghici, hitch3r,
Ela Kwasniewski, Sergey Nivens, Fedorov Oleksiy, Roman
Rybaleov, schankz, Dmitry Skutin, studioflara, Ronald Sumners,
TwilightArtPictures, wacpan), SuperStock (age fotostock),
Veer (marcus miranda)

LIBRARY OF CONGRESS
CATALOGING-IN-PUBLICATION DATA
Riggs, Kate.
Guitar / Kate Riggs.
p. cm. — (Making music)
SUMMARY: *A primary prelude to the guitar, including what the string*
instrument looks and sounds like, basic instructions on how to play it, and
the kinds of music that feature it.
Includes bibliographical references and index.

ISBN 978-1-60818-368-5 (*hardcover*)
ISBN 978-0-89812-947-2 (*pbk*)
1. Guitar—Juvenile literature. 1. Title.

ML1015.G9R54 2013
787.87—DC23   2013009495

HC 9 8 7 6 5 4 3 2
PBK 9 8 7 6 5 4 3

TABLE OF CONTENTS

WHEN YOU HEAR A GUITAR

Sparkling snow on a winter's day.

Ripping a hole in a pair of jeans.

A hot, crackling fire.

What do you think of when you hear a guitar?

Snow falls softly and quietly.
A warm fire can make you feel calm and safe.

THE STRING FAMILY

Musical instruments that sound and look

alike belong to a "family."

Guitars are members of the string family.

Most guitars have six strings.

The strings **vibrate** when you pluck them.

Strings cross the sound hole on some kinds of guitars.

guitar

banjo

mandolin

ukulele

lute

sitar

harp

violin

viola

cello

double bass

The lute was a popular instrument hundreds of years ago in Europe.

PARTS OF A GUITAR

The guitar looks a lot like the violin.

It probably came from an earlier string instrument

called the lute. The curved body of a guitar is usually

made of wood. The body can be hollow or solid.

The neck of a guitar sticks out from the top of the body.

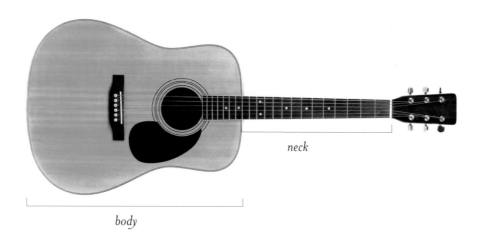

neck

body

FRETS AND STRINGS

The fingerboard is on top of the neck.

Metal strips called frets are found on the fingerboard.

A guitar's strings are stretched from

the bridge across the fingerboard.

The strings are made of **nylon** or steel.

fret

The frets help a guitarist play chords, or groups of notes.

tuning key

Guitar strings are tightened or loosened with tuning keys in the "head."

An electric guitar's body has sharper corners than an acoustic guitar's.

KINDS OF GUITARS

There are two main kinds of guitars.

Classical guitars are also called acoustic (*uh-KOO-stik*)

guitars. These guitars have hollow bodies.

Electric guitars have solid bodies. They use parts

called **pickups** to make loud sounds. Electric bass guitars

make lower sounds than regular electric guitars.

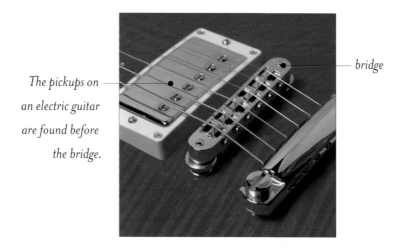

The pickups on an electric guitar are found before the bridge.

bridge

PLAYING THE GUITAR

Guitarists who sit down hold the guitar in their lap.

Guitarists who stand use a strap to support the guitar.

You hold the neck of the guitar with your left hand.

Then you pluck the strings with the fingers

of your right hand. Some guitarists

use a plectrum, or pick, instead of their fingers.

plectrum

Some guitarists wear picks on their thumb and fingers.

Singers in 1600s England sometimes played baroque guitars.

EARLY GUITARS

Guitars were first popular in Spain

hundreds of years ago. The baroque (*bah-ROKE*)

guitar was smaller than today's guitars.

Its frets were tied around the neck.

It had pairs of strings instead of single strings.

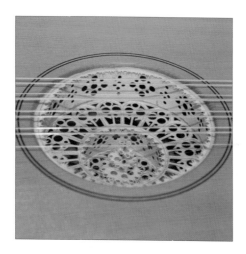

There were often five pairs of strings on a baroque guitar.

GUITAR MUSIC

Many types of music use guitars.

Guitarists play music by themselves.

Or they play with groups such as rock or country bands.

Some guitarists play with orchestras (*OR-keh-struhz*).

Many guitarists sing and play guitar at the same time.

TWO GUITARISTS PLAY

Two guitarists take the stage with their band.

The lead guitarist's fingers fly up and down the frets!

The bass guitarist picks a

steady beat as people sing along!

Heavy metal guitarist Wolf Hoffmann plays a V-shaped guitar.

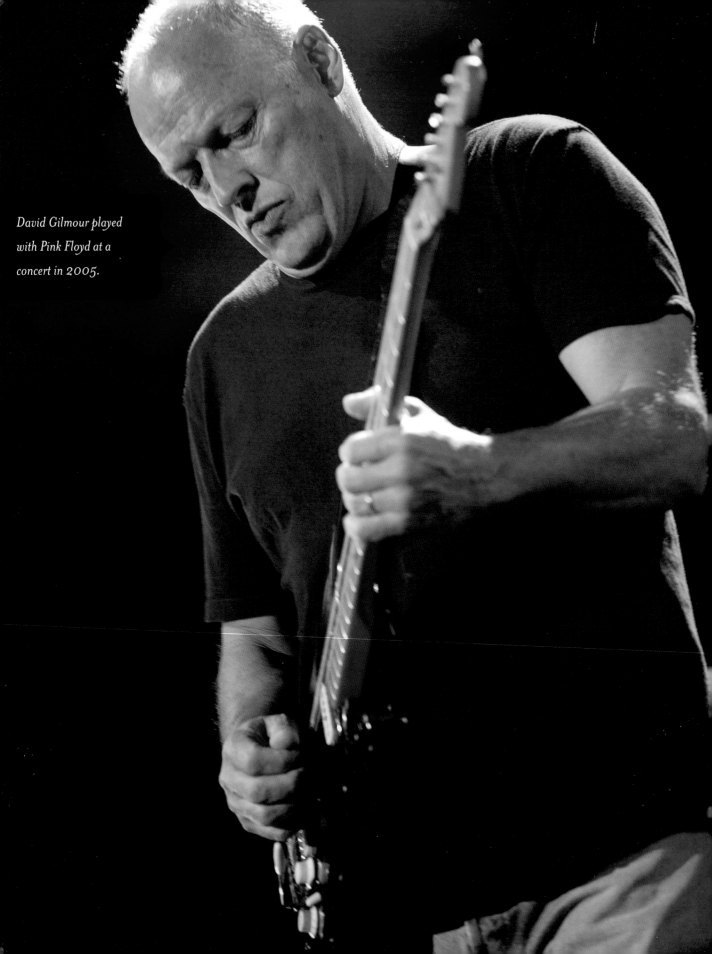

David Gilmour played with Pink Floyd at a concert in 2005.

MEET A GUITARIST

David Gilmour was born in 1946. He grew up in England.

David started playing guitar with a rock band

named Pink Floyd in 1968. The main electric guitar

he uses is called a Stratocaster.

It is black and was made by the Fender company.

David has played with many musicians over the years.

He also likes to play music to raise money for **charities***.*

GLOSSARY

charities: *groups that work to help other people*

nylon: *a tough, stretchy material*

pickups: *parts on electric guitars that send a string's sound to an amplifier, which makes the sound louder*

vibrate: *to shake or move up and down rapidly*

READ MORE

Bacon, Tony. *2,000 Guitars.*
San Diego, Calif.: Thunder Bay Press, 2009.

Ganeri, Anita. *Stringed Instruments.*
North Mankato, Minn.: Smart Apple Media, 2012.

Storey, Rita. *The Violin and Other Stringed Instruments.*
North Mankato, Minn.: Smart Apple Media, 2010.

WEBSITES

Adams Guitar
http://www.adamsguitar.com/
Click on a guitar, then use your computer keyboard to play it!

Enchanted Learning: Make a Box Guitar
http://www.enchantedlearning.com/crafts/
Boxguitar.shtml
Learn how to make your own guitar out of a shoebox or Kleenex box.

Every effort has been made to ensure that these sites are suitable for children, that they have educational value, and that they contain no inappropriate material. However, because of the nature of the Internet, it is impossible to guarantee that these sites will remain active indefinitely or that their contents will not be altered.